The Wise H

Tales and allegories of three contemporary sages

Through words and letters
We touch upon that hidden realm called
"The Spiritual World"

Laitman Kabbalah Publishers

THE WISE HEART:
TALES AND ALLEGORIES OF THREE CONTEMPORARY SAGES

Copyright © 2010 by MICHAEL LAITMAN

Published by Laitman Kabbalah Publishers
www.kabbalah.info   info@kabbalah.info
1057 Steeles Avenue West, Suite 532, Toronto, ON, M2R 3X1, Canada
Bnei Baruch USA, 2009 85th street, #51, Brooklyn, NY 11214, USA
Printed in Canada

Library of Congress Cataloging-in-Publication Data

Laitman, Michael.

The wise heart : tales and allegories of three contemporary sages / Michael Laitman ; compiled by Yael Lior. ~ 1st ed.

    p. cm.

ISBN: 978-1-897448-47-2

1. Jewish parables. 2. Jewish legends. 3. Spiritual life~Judaism. 4. Cabala. I. Li'or, Ya'el. II. Title. III. Title: Tales and allegories of three contemporary sages.

BM530.L25 2010

296.1'9~dc22   2010035351

Translation: Susan Gal

Copy Editor: Claire Gerus

Illustrations, Internal Design, and Cover Design: Yael Lior

Layout: Baruch Khovov

Printing: Grauer Printing LTD

Post Production: Uri Laitman

Executive Editor: Chaim Ratz

FIRST EDITION: August 2011

First printing

TABLE OF CONTENTS

Focus on the Creator

Based on a lecture by Michael Laitman (July 24, 2007)

The wisdom of Kabbalah shows us
How to turn ourselves around from within
To discover the Creator.

When zooming in on an object through a camera lens,
We turn the ring a little to the right, then a little to the left,
And sharpen our focus
Until suddenly,
There it is!
Our object is crystal clear.

In much the same way, we approach the Creator
By studying the wisdom of Kabbalah.

Spiritual Waves

Based on a lecture by Michael Laitman (July 24, 2007)

Our inner work is
To tune our hearts
And our senses
To perceive the spiritual world.

Like a radio receiver
On which the knobs are gently turned
To detect the waves in the air,
We tune ourselves
To the spiritual frequency
With increasing precision,
Using actions called "intentions."

Until suddenly,
Another dimension appears,
Disclosing the spiritual world.

A Small World

Based on a lecture by Michael Laitman (October 20, 2000)

A small child inhabits a small world.
He does not see,
Perceive,
Or understand
That a much larger world exists.

Even in his small world
He is told
That part of it is his to use,
And that other parts are not allowed.

But little by little
These boundaries
Expand,
And he begins to understand
That he is allowed to do more.

And the world he used to see
As a little bubble
Gradually expands.

He notices there is a street,
And a town beyond the street,
And there is the whole world.
And he himself on earth.

Similarly,
The wisdom of Kabbalah
Is gradually revealed to us.

The Worm in the Radish

Based on an allegory by Baal HaSulam in "Introduction to The Book of Zohar"

The worm born inside a radish
Sits there thinking
That the Creator's world
Is as bitter,
Dark,
And small
As the radish
In which it was born.

But as soon as the worm
Breaks through the radish's p
And gets a glimpse of the out
It says in wonderment,
"I thought the entire world
Was the size of the radish in which I was born,
But now I see
A great,
Bright,
And truly beautiful world
Before me."

An Airplane in the Sky

Based on an allegory by Rabash in *Letters of Rabash*, "Letter no. 37"

Ten people are standing,
Looking at an airplane in the distance.
Its size
In their eyes
Is just a tiny speck.

Some of the people have binoculars,
Showing the plane as much larger.
But each of them has a different kind of binoculars.
One set of binoculars greatly magnifies the plane,
While the other magnifies it less.

Therefore, one viewer sees
A four-meter airplane,
And the other says it's only three.
Yet another claims it is only two.

They are all telling
The truth about what they see,
But the differences among them
Make no changes to the plane itself.
Rather, the only differences are in the people
Looking at the airplane.

Walking Before the King

An allegory by Baal HaSulam from *A Sage's Fruit*, Letters, p 126

A man walking along the road
Sees a most beautiful garden
And hears a voice calling him.
It is the King strolling in the garden.

Excited,
The man leaps over the fence
And into the garden.
In his excitement and haste
He does not notice
That he is walking ahead of the King
While the King is strolling
Close behind him.

And so the man walks on,
Thanking the King and praising him
With all his heart
In preparation for
Greeting the King.
And still, he takes no notice
That the King is right beside him.

Suddenly, he turns around
And sees the King beside him.
Naturally, he is very glad
And he begins to walk behind the King,
Thanking and praising him with all his might,
For the King is ahead of him and he is behind.

And so they stroll right up to the entrance.
The man walks out the door,
Returning to his starting point,
And the King remains in the garden
And locks the gate.

When the man realizes
They have parted,
And that the King is no longer with him,
He begins to seek the opening of the garden
through which he had left,
So that the King will be ahead of him.

But there is no such gate.
There is only the way
He entered the first time,
When he was ahead of the King.
And the King was behind him,
Undetected.

The Point in the Heart

Based on a lecture by Michael Laitman (October 5, 2007)

For tens of thousands of years
We evolve
In this world.
Until suddenly,
The point in our hearts awakens
That recollection called,
"A part of God above."

Then we begin to ask,
"What is the meaning of my life?"
And to long for something
Higher than this world.

A Building with an Elevator

Based on a lecture by Michael Laitman (December 22, 2000)

Reality is a permanent structure.
It is like a building
With 125 floors
And an elevator to go up and down.
It goes up wherever one wishes
And down to where one descends.

Besides the person,
Nothing else changes.
He is the operator of the elevator
Going up or down in the building.

This elevator is the heart in each of us,
The conditions of our hearts,
And all we need is to search
How to ride up,
And then *desire*
To ride up.

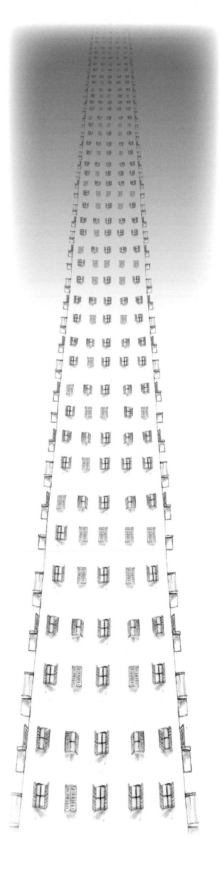

Revealed On the Outside

From Letter no. 35 in "Letters of Rabash"

When the heart is filled
With excitement,
Whether it is caused by good things
Or by bad things,
The impression is revealed on the outside.
It is like a glass of water:
When it's full,
It overflows.
Likewise, our tears
Are the overflowing surplus.

The Right Scrutiny

Based on a lecture by Michael Laitman (February 15, 2007)

Every step of the way,
Wherever we turn,
We must scrutinize.

Our scrutiny is
To rise
Above emotion and above reason
Requesting the reason of the Upper One.

The reason of the Upper One
Is called "Faith and Bestowal"
Whereas man's reason
Is called "Knowing and Receiving."

A Diamond on Sale

An allegory by Rabash in *Steps of the Ladder*, Vol. 1, Article no. 55

Once, some people purchased a diamond
And were joyful that they had paid
An extremely low price.
But one of them wondered
If, in fact, the diamond was genuine.

No one in town knew
Anything about diamonds,
So they went to an expert merchant
To find out if
The diamond was real or fake.
They were pleased with his reply
That it was real.

But one man wondered
About trusting the merchant,
Since he might be a crook himself.
So this man decided to learn
The trade himself
And become an expert,
Which he did, successfully.

Gold Coins

Based on the Ari's "The Tree of Life," p. 125, Chapter 5

Once a king wished to send
A large sum of gold coins
To his son,
Who was on a faraway island.

But alas, all the people in his kingdom
Were thieves and crooks
And he had no trusted servants.

What did he do?

He exchanged the coins
For small change
And sent the money
To his son,
Borne by many servants.
In this way, such a theft
Would not be worth
Blemishing the honor
Of the kingdom.

The Servant and the Ministers

Based on an allegory by Baal HaSulam in *A Sage's Fruit*, Letters (p 25)

Once there was a king
Who was so fond of his servant,
He wished to make the servant
Superior to all his ministers.
He recognized the great,
Unfailing love within his servant's heart.

But it was not kinglike
To promote a person
All at once
For no apparent reason.

Rather, the proper manner for a king
Is to disclose his reasons to all,
Revealing his profound wisdom.

What did the King do?

He appointed his servant
To guard his very own castle.
He also told one of the ministers,
A gifted comic,
To pretend he was a rebel
Against the kingdom,
And to attack the castle
When the king's guards were unprepared.

The minister did as he was told.
With great resourcefulness and shrewdness
He pretended to assail the king's castle.

The servant, now guarding the castle,
Risked his life and saved the king.
He fought the minister
With unrelenting bravery
Until all could plainly see
His love and loyalty
To his king.

Then, the minister removed his costume
And all laughed with glee
(As the servant had fought with all his might
Only to discover it was all
Imaginary and completely unreal).

They laughed even more
When the minister told
Of his imaginary character,
Deeply cruel at heart,
And of the great fear
He was sure he had seen.

And every detail
In this dreadful struggle
Brought a round of laughter and great joy.

But even so,
The servant was still a servant,
And unschooled, as well.
How could he be made superior
To all the king's ministers and servants?

The king pondered this question,
And as before, commanded the same minister
To pretend he was a robber and a murderer
And wage a bitter war against him.

The king was certain
That in the second war,
He would reveal to his servant a wondrous wisdom,
Enough to make him worthy
Of leading all the ministers.

And so the king appointed the servant
To guard the kingdom's treasure.
And that same minister dressed up
As a vicious murderer
Set out to steal the king's secret riches.

The poor guard
Fought once more with all his might
And with complete devotion
Until his quota was filled.

Then the minister took off his costume
And there was great joy
In the king's palace,

Even more so than before
As the details of the minister's tricks
Brought about great laughter.

Since now he had to exhibit
Even further wisdom and craftiness.

Because it was now evident
That there was no cruelty whatsoever
In the kingdom,
And those they thought were cruel
Were only jokers.

In fact, that minister needed great ingenuity
To convincingly appear as a villain.

The Birth of a Blissful Humanity

From *A Sage's Fruit*, Essays, "The Secret of Conception and Birth," by Baal HaSulam

Our development in Creation
Is nothing other than our mimicry of it,
As the very feel and beauty
Of the colors we design and innovate
Are nothing other than copies of the appealing colors
That we find in flowers.

Take a carpenter, for instance,
How would he know how to make a four-legged table
If he hadn't copied the work of the Creator,
Who created four-legged creatures?

How would he know how to join two pieces of wood,
If not by imitating the way our limbs are joined,
And putting the pieces of wood together accordingly?

That's what people do.
They look and learn as best they can
In order to understand reality,
Which is set before them
In its perfect beauty.

When all of that is understood,
People make replicas.
That sample then becomes the basis for another sample
Until man has created a lovely world
Full of inventions.

Based on the observation of the work of Creation,
Planes have been built resembling a flying bird.
Radios have been made to perceive sound waves,
Just like ears.

In short,
Everything we've succeeded in doing
Has been set before us in Creation.
In our reality, exactly as it is,
Nothing is missing,
Except to learn from it
And create accordingly.

Spiritual Birth

From *A Sage's Fruit*, Essays, "The Secret of Conception and Birth," by Baal HaSulam

Just as there are births from bodies,
There is birth by renewal of the spiritual force,
When we reach the world of correction.

Similar to a physical embryo,
Born from its mother's womb,
We come from a dark
And corrupt world,
Unclean and unpleasant,
Into a bright and perfect world:
The world of correction.

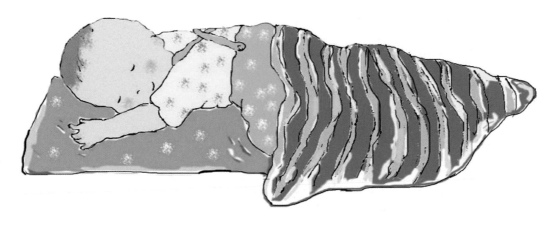

In corporeality,
The newborn
Slides into the loving arms
Of caring parents,
Who ensure its existence and well-being.
Similarly, once each of us
Is given 600,000 who
Care for our existence,
We all breathe the breath of life
As one man in one heart.

Breathing Air

From *Steps of the Ladder*, Vol 1, Article no. 274, by Rabash

We see
That people must constantly
Breathe air,
Or they will lose their lives.
And this air must go back and forth,
Meaning, after inhaling,
He must exhale
And immediately inhale again.

The air previously inhaled
Is useful only for a moment.
And if we wish to go on living,
We must immediately
Inhale fresh air.

Earth's Pull

Based on a lecture by Michael Laitman (October 31, 2006)

All matter of Creation
Holds the desire to receive,
The desire for pleasure,
Matter drawing towards itself.

The Earth pulls,
Plus attracts minus.
All of the forces
And magnetic fields
Are kinds of pulling forces.

Our thoughts
Have a pulling force, as well.
Since man
Is made entirely of matter that pulls,
He constantly desires,
And yearns to fill himself.

Subconsciously,
He always calculates
What is to his benefit,
How to avoid harm,
And how to attract good.

The Earth Bore Its Fruit

From *Letters of Rabash*, Letter no. 37

The Earth bears fruit,
Receiving strength
From the rain, wind, and sun.

If she lacks one of the forces
That she needs,
She does not bear,
Does not bestow,
And cannot create a thing.
And then people can't be nourished by her.

Rather, tragically,
They could become extinct
From starvation,
If the Earth did not
Bear fruit.

But when man
Sows and plants and reaps,
She reciprocates accordingly.
The way man serves the Earth
Is the way the Earth serves man.

Rain Upon the Earth

An allegory by Baal HaSulam in *A Sage's Fruit*, Discussions (p126)

Just as rain is sent
Onto the Earth,
And the Earth can't sense
Who sent it,
Man is utterly incapable
Of sensing who sent him a thought
Because he cannot sense it
Until it has arrived
In his mind.
And once it is in his possession,
It seems like a part of his being.

Correcting Nature

From *Steps of the Ladder*, vol. 2 article no. 822, by Rabash

Nature can't be changed,
But man can use his nature
For the purpose of
Correcting the world.

This means that he can use each and every trait
In a way that brings correction to the world,
Rather than its destruction,
Similar to matters concerning the physical world.

For example, it is commonly known
That fire is harmful.
If a fire breaks out,
It devours and burns bodies and property.

However, at the same time,
When we use fire as needed,
It brightens the night,
It heats our houses in winter,
And it cooks our food.

So we can see
That even with the most harmful thing,
If used for correction,
Can result in the world
Enjoying fire,
Rather than fleeing it.

A Perfect Machine

Based on a lecture by Michael Laitman (December 15, 2006)

People can be happy
Only when connected
To the entire machine.

To the extent of disconnection
We aren't nourished from its perfection.

The machine is perfect,
Since it is operated by
The law of unconditional giving.
And we must adhere to that law
As inseparable parts of that machine.

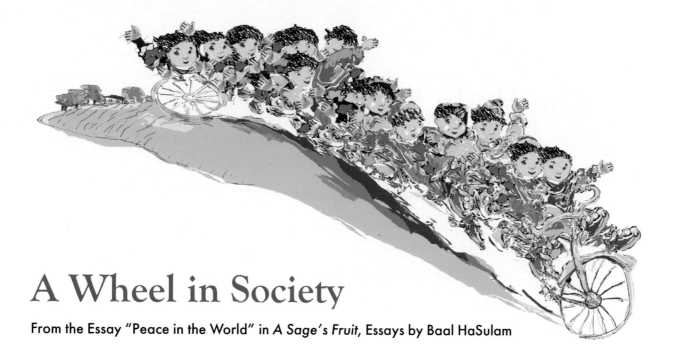

A Wheel in Society

From the Essay "Peace in the World" in *A Sage's Fruit*, Essays by Baal HaSulam

Man was created
To lead a social life.
Each and every individual
Is like a wheel,
Joined with numerous others,
All placed on one machine.

A single wheel
Has no freedom of motion
In and of itself.
Rather,
It follows the motion
Of the rest of the wheels
In a certain direction,
For the machine
To do its task.

And if one of the wheels is broken,
It isn't evaluated or measured
In relation to itself,
But rather
In relation to its function and service
Of the entire machine.

The Body Knows

An allegory by Baal HaSulam in "A Speech for the Completion of the Zohar"

When the whole body thinks
That one of its organs
Can serve and please it,
That organ immediately knows
The thought
And provides the intended pleasure.

Similarly, if a certain organ thinks and senses
That its place is too narrow,
The entire body instantly knows
Its thought and sensation,
And moves it to a place of comfort.

However, if it should happen
That a certain organ
Is detached from the body,
They become two separate entities,
And the body no longer
Knows the needs
Of that separate organ.
And likewise, the organ doesn't know
The body's thoughts
Through which to serve it.

Drawing by Rav Iaitman, January 15, 2008

And should a doctor come
And reattach the organ to the body as before,
Then the organ will once again know
The thoughts and needs
Of the whole body
And the whole body will know once more
The needs of the organ.

The Body of the Nation

Based on "The Nation" by Baal HaSulam

Each person
Must find perfect harmony
Among his organs.

The eyes see,
And the brain assists them
To think and to advise,
And then the hands work
Or fight,
And the feet walk.
Thus, each is ready and
Awaits its call to duty.

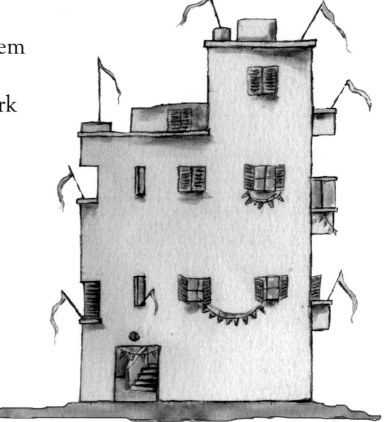

Similarly are the organs
That form the core of the Nation.
The advisers, employers,
Employees, and leaders
Must operate in perfect harmony.
It is essential for the Nation's proper living
And for its secure existence.

The Force of Multiplicity

From *A Sage's Fruit*, Essays, "The Secret of Conception and Birth," by Baal HaSulam

In the world
Is a spiritual force,
Unique and wondrous.

Accordingly,
Any holism is
Praiseworthy and appealing,
Since it stems from
The spiritual force.

Each individualism
Is low and contemptible.

This difference distinguishes
Between the self-centered individual
And one who is devoted to his nation.

Thus, the first moral is
That being devoted to one's nation
Is more important than being devoted to one's town,
And being devoted to the world
Is more important than being devoted to one's nation.

The Shopkeeper Sells on Credit

From "The Peace" by Baal HaSulam

Rabbi Akiva said,
"Everything is temporary
And that a fortress surrounds all of life.

The shop is open
And the owner gives credit.
The book is open
And the hand writes.
And whoever wishes to borrow
May borrow.

The collectors call frequently,
Every day.
And the debts are paid,
Knowingly and unknowingly.
They can be assured
The judgment is just
And all is prepared for the feast."

A Drop in Value

From "Take a Priestly Tithe from Your Produce to the Lord,"
from *Steps of the Ladder*, vol. 1 by Rabash

In corporeal decline,
We sometimes see
That it is stated
That the value of gold has dropped
And it is not as significant

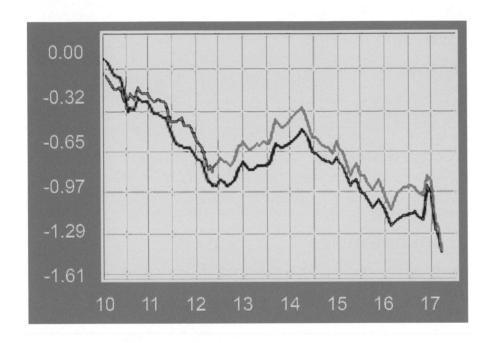

As it should be.
So it is in spirituality.
If it doesn't have the value
That it should,
No one pays
For what it costs.

The Recipient of the Gift

From "What Is a True Grace, in the Work?" in *The Rungs of the Ladder*, by Rabash

We know
That when the recipient of a gift
Praises the gift that his friend gave him,
His friend enjoys it even more.

But if the recipient of the gift tells him:
"I have no need for the gift you gave me,"
His friend will surely not be pleased.

On the contrary,
The more the recipient
Feels a need for the gift,
The more the giver is pleased.
It is expressed in the measure
Of gratitude that the recipient
Gives back to the giver.

Hence, the more
We try to enjoy
The delight and the pleasure
That the Creator gave us,
The more there is contentment Above,
From the recipient's increased pleasure.

The Gift of Grace

Based on an allegory by Baal HaSulam in the Essay "The Giving of the Torah"

A rich man once gathered a person from the market.
He gave him food and drink
And showered him with silver and gold
And other valuables each day.
And every day his gifts surpassed
The gifts of the previous day,
Continuing on and on.

Finally, the rich man asked,
"Tell me, have all your wishes been fulfilled?"
And the man replied, "Not all my wishes have been fulfilled,
For how good and how delighted I would be
If all of these valuables
Came to me through my own efforts
As they came to you,
And I would not be receiving gifts at your grace."

Then the rich man replied,
"In that case, never has a man been created
Who can fulfill your wishes."

All is Measured
according to the Vessel

Based on an Allegory from Steps of the Ladder, *Vol. 2, Article no. 856*

A father gives his young son
A penny a day.

If his love for his son grows,
And he wishes to make him happy
And give him five cents,
The child sees
That he has now received a larger gift.

Surely he will admiringly wish
To praise and thank
His father for that.

But if later on
His father chooses to give him
One penny as before,
His son will fill with anger at his father
For the smaller amount he has now received.

It follows that
Yesterday's bonus
Was not enough to bring him closer.
Rather, by the father increasing his goodness,
The son has become farther from his father,
Since in his mind,
His father is obligated and must increase his gifts daily.

Father Creates Vessels

Based on an allegory by Baal HaSulam from *Shamati*, Article no. 33

Consider a person
Whose trade is to create clay vases and vessels.

First, he makes round balls of clay,
And then he carves holes in the balls.

When his young son
Sees what his father is doing
He cries out:
"Father, why are you ruining the balls?"

His son does not realize
That his father's main intent
Is the holes,
As only they can be filled and receive.
But the son wishes to fill the holes
That his father made in the balls.

An allegory of a Tiny Vessel

Based on an allegory by Baal HaSulam from *Shamati*, Article no. 52

What does one do if he wishes to give his friend
A barrel full of wine,
But his friend has only a tiny cup?

He pours wine into that cup,
And his friend takes it home
And empties it there.

Then he returns with the cup
Fills it with wine once more,
And again returns to his home,
Until he receives all the barrels of wine.

I heard another tale.
Once there were two friends,
One of whom became a king,
And the other a pauper.

When he heard that his friend
Had become a king,
The pauper approached his friend, the king,
And told him of his misfortune.

So the king gave him
A letter for the treasurer,
Allowing him two hours to take
As much money as he wanted.

The pauper went to the treasury
With a tiny box.
He entered and filled his tiny box with money.
But as he was leaving,
The clerk kicked the box
And all the money fell to the ground.

And so it happened again and again.
And the pauper cried,
"Why are you treating me this way?"

Finally, the clerk told him:
"All the money you have taken
All this time
Is yours.
You may take it all.
Because you had no vessel
With which to take enough money from the treasury,
I played this trick on you."

The Master's Trusted Servant

An allegory by Baal HaSulam from "Introduction to The Study of the Ten Sefirot," Item 108

This is a story
About a man, a trusted servant
Of a certain master,
Whom the master loved as himself.

One time,
The master went away,
Leaving his business in the hands of his substitute,
A man who hated the servant.

What did he do?
He took the servant
And whipped him five lashes
In public for all to see,
To degrade him and humiliate him.

When the master returned,
The servant approached him
And told him what had happened.
The master was infuriated.

He called for his substitute
And ordered him to immediately give the servant
One thousand coins for each whipping.
The servant took the money and returned to his home.

His wife found him weeping,
Anxiously she said:
"What happened between you and the master?"
He told her.

She asked, "So why are you crying?"
He replied, "I am crying because
He whipped me only five lashes.
I wish he had whipped me
At least ten lashes,
Since now I would have
Ten thousand coins."

A Voice Calls Unto Him

Based on an allegory by Baal HaSulam from *Shamati*, Article no. 241

If one is lost in the thick woods,
If he does not see any way out
To reach a town,
He becomes desperate,
And thinks he will never return home.

When he sees someone from a distance
Or hears someone's voice,
His desire to return home will instantly revive as before,
And he will begin to yell and cry out for someone
To come and save him.

It is likewise with one who has lost
The good path, and
Entered an evil place,
And has grown accustomed
To living among vicious animals.
If he hears the voice calling out to him,
He awakens to repent
For this is the voice of the Creator, not his own.

Thus, when the Creator
Wishes to lead us out of the dense forest
He shows us a glitter from afar.
Then the person musters what strength he has left
To walk on the path towards the glitter, in order to reach it.

Only the Heroes

An allegory by Baal HaSulam from "Introduction to The Study of the Ten Sefirot," Item 133

Once, a king wished to select
All of his most loyal and loving subjects in the country
And bring them to work inside his palace.
What did he do?
He issued a decree across the land,
That anyone who so desired,
Big and small,
Would come to him
And engage in work inside his palace.

But he positioned many of his servants
As guards at the gate of the palace,
And on all the roads leading to his palace.
He ordered them to cunningly mislead
All those who came close to his palace,
And to divert them from the road that led to the palace.

Naturally, all the people of the kingdom
Started running to the king's castle,
But they were turned away by the diligent guards.
Yet, many overcame them
And succeeded in getting closer to the castle's gate.

Still, the guards at the gate were most diligent,
And whomever approached the gate
Was driven off with great shrewdness,
Until the people left as they had arrived.

The Wise Heart

And so they came and went, and came and went,
regained their strength and came again, time after time
For days and years on end
Until they tried no more.

And only the heroes among them
Whose patience had held up
defeated those guards
And opened the gate.
And they were instantly greeted by the king,
Who appointed each to
The suitable position.

Of course, from then on,
They had no dealings
With the guards
Who had discouraged them and driven them away,
Making their lives bitter
For days and years on end,
Making them run back and forth to the gate.
For they had been rewarded with working and serving
Before the glorious light, the king's face,
Inside his palace.

The Difference between Envy and Lust

From *Steps of the Ladder*, Article no. 154, by Rabash

There once was a greedy man,
Who coveted everything he saw,
And a jealous man,
Who always envied what others owned,
Although he needed nothing.

They walked along together.
On the way, the king met them.
He said, "One of you
Shall ask something of me,
And I will grant it;
Then I will give the other
Double."

The greedy one desired both parts.
Hence, he did not wish to be the first to ask.
And the other didn't wish to ask first, either,
As he would be jealous of his friend
If he received twice what he, himself, was given.

Finally, the greedy one urged the envious one
To ask first.
What did the envious one do?
He asked for one of his eyes to be blinded,
So the king would give the greedy one double,
blinding both his eyes.

The Evil Attributes

Based on the essay, "Peace in the World," by Baal HaSulam

As the Creator meticulously
Watches over all the details
Of His Creation,
Not letting anyone
Destroy anything He owns,
But turn it around
And reform it.

Hence, all of the "world reformers"
Will vanish from the earth,
And all the evil attributes in the world
Will remain on the earth.

The evil things exist,
And comprise the number of
Degrees of development
They must undergo
Until they are fully ripened.

And then
Those evil attributes will
Turn themselves around,
And become good and helpful attributes,
Just as the Creator had planned from the beginning.

This is akin to a fruit
On the branch of a tree
Awaiting and counting the days
And the months
It must endure
Until it is fully ripe.
At that time, its savor and sweetness
Will be revealed to every person.

Seeing the Sounds

Based on a letter of Baal HaSulam from *A Sage's Fruit*, Letters, (p 85)

Sound and tremor
Are one and the same,
But not all sounds
Can be pleasant.

The sound of thunder is frightening,
Unpleasant to the human ear,
Since the tremor takes up
Much of the power of its blow,
And also too much time.
Even if the blow were small,
It would still irritate the ear
For it would last too long.

But the sound of the violin
Is pleasant to the listener,
Since the force of the strike is measured
And its time is accurately measured, too.
One who extends the time
Ruins the pleasantness.

Healing the Sick

An allegory by Rabash from *The Rungs of the Ladder*

Imagine a person
Who had someone ill in his household.
What would he do?
He would go to the doctor and ask of
The doctor to be a good emissary of the Creator,
And heal the sick one.

But if, tragically, he has not yet healed,
Normally, he would
Turn to a professor.
Then he'd say,
Surely *he* will be a good emissary of the Creator
And will heal the sick one.

And if the professor could not help as well,
Then the professors might deliberate,
Perhaps together, through their consultation,
They would find some remedy for the ill one.

If that still did not help,
Then they would naturally
Turn to the Creator and say,
"Dear Lord, if You don't help me,
No one will help me.
We have already been to all of the great doctors,
Who are Your emissaries,
And not one could help me.
I have no one to turn to except You,
For You to help me."

And then, when he is healed,
The person says,
"Only the Creator himself helped me,"
And not through an emissary.

The Power of Strength

From "Introduction to The Tree of Life" by Baal HaSulam

We find qualitative power in strength,
As in lions and leopards
Whose quality of power of their strength,
Deters all people from fighting them.

Whereas in others
We find power and strength
Without any quality at all, but
Rather quantity alone,
Such as in flies.

As a result of their multiplicity
No man will fight them.
These wanderers walk freely
In people's homes
And on set tables,
And people feel weak
Compared to them.

That is not so
With other unwanted guests,

Such as field flies, insects and the like,
Although their force is of greater quality
Than that of house flies.

People will not rest or be at ease,
Until the last one is driven out.
That is because nature
Did not endow them
With the force of multiplicity,
Like flies.

The Train of Development

Based on a lecture by Michael Laitman (October 21, 2003)

In this world, our lives
Resemble a person sitting in a train,
Racing from point A to point B.
And even though he wants to stay at point A,
The train continues to point B.

The nearer he comes to point B
The more he feels pulled to return to point A,
But he sees that
He keeps moving further from point A,
And this distance is sensed by him
As suffering.

A Short Path and a Long Path

Based on a lecture by Michael Laitman (July 24, 2007)

"Short" and "long"
Do not refer to the path itself.

The stages along the path
Are the same in both,
Yet are experienced differently.

It's like traveling to Jerusalem.
Once people used to go up to Jerusalem
With a horse and cart,
And the journey took several days.
There were overnight stops,
Robbers along the way,
And by the time you got there you were sick and hungry.

And today
The same road is traveled in no time.
You get in the car,
And you're in Jerusalem within 45 minutes.

The Unique Role of a Kabbalist

Based on a TV interview with Michael Laitman

A Kabbalist does not reincarnate and come to the world,
For his own needs.
Rather, he has a unique role:
To build the system
In order to bring the Upper Lights
Closer to the people of his generation.
He is a mediator between the spiritual Light
And the people who are at the corporeal level of
perception,
Disconnected from this Light.

This system has many degrees,
And the Kabbalists act systematically.
Kabbalists do everything for a reason,
And only after receiving permission from Above.
Then the Kabbalist prepares himself below,
To be adapted to his generation.

And until he completes the entire process
Of assembling the descent of the Lights downward
Into this world
According to the needs of the generation,
He does not feel
He has completed his task.

Kabbalah Books

Based on a lecture by Michael Laitman (October 13, 2006)

At the moment of Creation,
The will to receive was created,
Along with the system
For the corruption
And the correction of this will.

And within that system,
It is already enrooted
That there will be Kabbalists
Who will write books,
And that the knowledge of spirituality
Will reach people in this way.
And they will use the books
To return to the root.

The King's Seal

Based on a letter of Baal HaSulam from *A Sage's Fruit*, Letters, (p 85)

A person
Is a small world
Behaving according to the letters
Imprinted within.

Each letter
Is like a minister for a time,
Making evaluations,
And the King of the World signs them.
In the event of a letter
Erring in a certain program,
It instantly resigns from its office
And the King appoints another letter, instead.

At the end of correction
That letter called "Messiah"
Shall reign,
And will complete and connect all the generations.

The Letter *Bet* is for "Blessing"

From *The Book of Zohar*, "Introduction of The Book of Zohar,"
Essay, "Letters of Rav Hamnuna Saba," Item 3

The Letter *Bet* entered
And said to Him:
"Lord Almighty,
It is good for You to create the world with me,
Since through me You are blessed
From Above and below,
As *Bet* means blessing."

The Creator agreed
That its virtue was worthy
Of creating the world with it,
And He said:
"Certainly I will create the world with you,
Since the light of your blessing shines equally
Above and below,
And you will be the beginning
With which to Create the world."

Why is the letter *Bet* a good and sufficient beginning
To lead the world to ultimate wholeness?
Because it is the light of the blessing,
The Light of Mercy, which is the temple of the Light of
Wisdom.

This Light never dims at all
As it passes and cascades through the degrees.
Just as it receives from Infinity at the highest degree,

One, Unique, and Unified

Based on *The Study of the Ten Sefirot*, Part One, "Inner Reflection," Item 8

In a single thought,
This entire reality
Was emanated and created,
The Upper and the lower alike

Until the end of time,
At the end of correction.

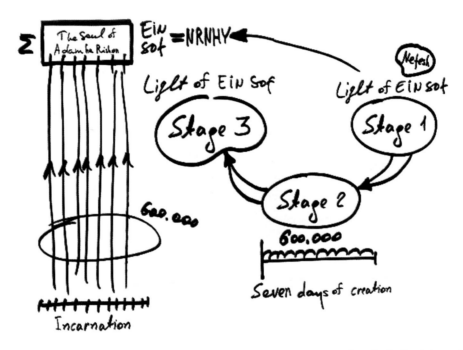

Drawing by Rav Laitman, November 27, 2007

And that single thought
Activates all,
It is the substance of all actions.
It is the purpose,
The essence of the effort,
And is itself perfection,
And the whole of the aspired reward.

The Quarry of the Soul

Based on *The Study of the Ten Sefirot*, Part One, "Inner Reflection," Item 3

The soul is a Divine part from Above.
Similar to a stone carved from the mountain,
The essence of the mountain
And the essence of the stone are the same,
And there no distinction between the stone and the mountain,
Except that the stone is a part of the mountain,
And the mountain is "the whole."

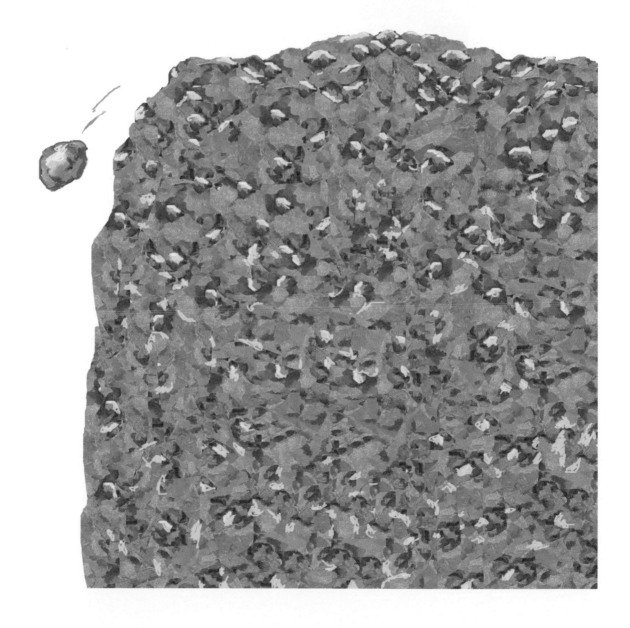

Ten Covers

From "Preface to the Sulam Commentary" Item 1, by Baal HaSulam

The sunlight
Cannot be looked at
Except through darkened glass,
Which decreases its light and makes it
Suitable for our eyes to see.

Quite similarly,
The lower ones would not be able to attain His Light
If their eyes were not covered with ten covers
Called "Ten *Sefirot*,"
Where each cover is beneath the other,
Further concealing His Light.

What is the Middle Line?

Based on an allegory by Rabash from *Steps of the Ladder*, Vol. 2, Article 544

A tale is told about two people
Who wished to hold a feast.
One said he would provide everything
Except for salt, vinegar, garlic, and the rest of the spices.
And the other would provide the spices.

In the end, they were in disagreement,
So each held his feast separately.
One provided flour, fish, meat, and herring,
And the other held a feast with all of the spices.

Which of the guests in either feast could enjoy the meal?
Spices alone cannot be enjoyed.
After all, who can eat salt, garlic, onions,
Black pepper or spicy greens alone?
Likewise, who can eat meat, fish or the like with no salt?

Thus, they had no choice
But to make peace
And hold both feasts together.
And they were delicious.

The Affliction of Divinity

Based on Article no. 156 *Steps of the Ladder*, Vol. 1

A king with a tower full of all the best,
But with no guests,
Is similar to one who held a wedding for his son,
Ordering hundreds of servings,
Although no guests arrived,
As there were none who wished to come
And enjoy what he had to offer from his tower.

The Son of the Great King

An allegory by Baal HaSulam from "Introduction to The Tree of Life"

A king who has
A tower full of all the best,
But with no guests,
Surely sits and awaits their arrival.
For if not,
All his preparations
Will have been in vain.

This is similar to a great king
Who bore a son in his latter years,
A son he loved more than anything.
So from the day the boy was born,
The king thought of good things for him.
He gathered all the books
And the wisest teachers in the country
And built for him a seminary for wisdom.

He assembled the finest builders
To build for him palaces of pleasure.
He summoned the greatest musicians
To build his son music halls.
He also gathered the best cooks and bakers
In the country
And provided him with every delicacy in the world.

Alas, the son grew up,
And lo, he was a fool.
He had no wish for education.

He was blind
And could not see or sense
The beauty of the buildings.
And he was deaf,
Unable to enjoy the voices of the singers.
And he was also diabetic,
Forbidden to eat
Anything but coarse-flour bread.
Indeed, an infuriating conclusion.

The Head of *Arich Anpin*

Based on a lecture by Michael Laitman (October 13, 2006)

The system of the head of *Arich Anpin*
Operates in order to bestow Lights,
To be our bestower.

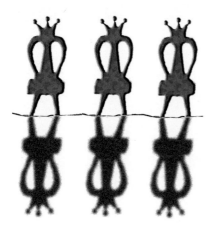

If a person desires to be the bestower,
Like that system,
To be an active part within it,

He studies the wisdom of Kabbalah.
And through this study,
He understands the operations of that system,
And how it bestows.

The Taste of Manna

Based on *The Study of the Ten Sefirot*, Part One, "Inner Reflection," Item 2

Let us learn from those who ate manna.
Manna is called "Heaven's bread,"
As it did not materialize
In this world.

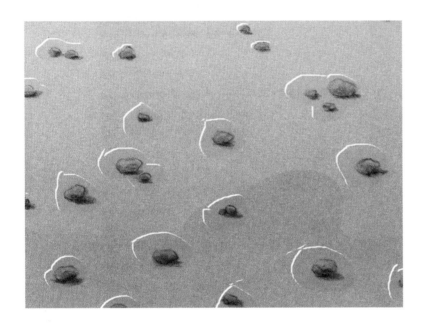

Our sages said
That each who tasted it
Found whatever they wished for,
Meaning it had to have consisted of
Opposite forms.
Thus, one might taste sweetness in it
While another would taste it as acrid and bitter.

Hence, the manna itself
Had to have consisted
Of both opposites at once.

Written in the Language of the Zohar

The Book of Zohar, Miketz (At the End), p 64

Come and see
Each and every day
When the sun rises.
A bird awakens
In a tree in the Garden of Eden,
And calls out three times.

And the herald calls aloud,
"Those among you who see
But do not see,
Who are in the next world
But do not know they exist,
They would be better off not to have been born
Than to be born."

This is because the wisdom of Kabbalah is before them,
And they do not engage in it
Or observe the glory of their Master.

Taste and See

Based on a lecture by Michael Laitman (July 24, 2007)

The Creator
Created one vessel
Called *Adam HaRishon*,
And shattered it
Into numerous tiny fragments.

He did this in order for them
To learn together
What it means to love,
And together reach
All the way to Him.

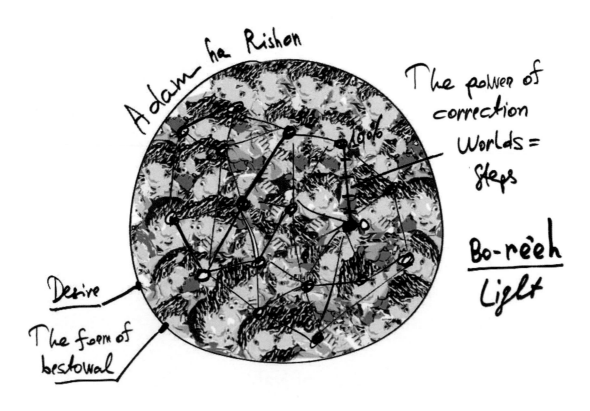

Based on a drawing by Rav Laitman, January 15, 2008

A Vessel for Abundance

An allegory by Rabash from *Steps of the Ladder*, Vol. 2, Article no. 856

Abundance itself
Is similar to a vast sea.

Some take from it
With a thimble,
While others
With a bucket.

On Two Levels

Based on a lecture by Michael Laitman (September 29, 2006)

Every thing and every concept
Should be interpreted on two levels:
The common level
And the level of truth.

The common level is entirely make-believe,
Like children playing with a toy car
As if it were a real car,
Or a toy plane
As if it were a real plane.

But the level called "truth"
Or "The wisdom of truth"
Is entirely real work.
And that is the level we must reach.

However, we need those forces
That raise us up
And bring us to that level.

Epilogue

Based on a lecture by Michael Laitman (January 01, 2008)

"It makes no difference how much a child understands. But from precisely that section that he reads and does not understand, the surrounding Light is drawn to him and keeps his soul.

At that time, that person is guaranteed to stay out of harm's way, as he is surrounded by a higher force than our world. This is why the wisdom of Kabbalah is the springboard for children and for people everywhere."

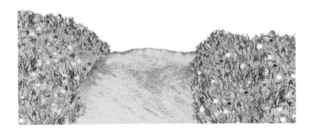